MW00848562

GALE
CENGAGE Learning

Novels for Students, Volume 57

Project Editor: Kristen A. Dorsch Rights Acquisition and Management: Ashley Maynard, Carissa Poweleit Composition: Evi Abou-El-Seoud

Manufacturing: Rita Wimberley

Imaging: John Watkins

Printed in Mexico
1 2 3 4 5 6 7 21 20 19 18 17

A Step from Heaven

An Na 2001

Introduction

A Step from Heaven is a youngadult novel that
follows Young Ju as she goes from being a toddler
in Korea to being the older sister in a family of
immigrants in America. The challenges of being
separated from relatives back home, adapting to life
in a new language, and starting educational and
professional life from scratch would be enough to
make life difficult for most families, but the Parks
face additional problems. The biggest problem
comes in the person of the domineering father, Apa,
who drinks alcohol to excess and abuses the people
closest to him. As Apa's oppressive, patriarchal
position increasingly clashes with Young Ju's

modern and liberal understanding of the world, tensions in the family mount, until some sort of resolution becomes absolutely necessary.

The novel's author, An Na, made her debut with *A Step from Heaven* in 2001 and has since written additional works oriented toward youngadult readers that have met with critical and popular acclaim. In her debut novel especially, she has in part drawn on her own experiences as a child in a family of immigrants. *A Step from Heaven* was a finalist for the National Book Award for Young People's Literature and won the Michael L. Printz Award, given by the American Library Association to the year's most outstanding youngadult novel, in 2002.

An Na was born on July 17, 1972, in South Korea. The experiences of Young Ju in A Step from Heaven are rooted in the framework of An Na's life, as she originally wrote many of the novel's episodes with express autobiographical intentions. For example, like her debut's protagonist, she had her hair permed before her family moved from Korea to San Diego, California. However, the fictional drama of the abusive father does not match her own family's experiences; she has related that her father was stern and had a traditional perspective, but together, despite the occasional arguments, her parents were able to adapt well to life in the United States. As a young child, An Na was already telling stories, using her stuffed animals—especially a bunny named Buggy who had half a dozen distinct personalities—to act them out. She became a devoted reader, spending hours at a time in the bathroom, the one room in her house with a lock, in order to absorb tales in full privacy. Her favorite authors included Laura Ingalls Wilder, whose famous Little House books functioned as primers on traditional American culture, as well as Beverly Cleary and Madeleine L'Engle.

As she grew into her teenage years, An Na came to inhabit a divided self. In school, surrounded by mostly white peers whose occasional comments on her racial differences led her to avoid attracting notice, she was a quiet achiever who declined to raise her hand in class and spoke little in social settings. The place where her true inner self emerged was her church, where she became joyful, buoyant, and outgoing in being surrounding by friends who were also Korean and who could offer sympathetic ears with regard to the challenges in her daily life.

After graduating in 1994 from Amherst College in Massachusetts, An Na enrolled in the Master of Fine Arts program in children's literature at Vermont College in Montpelier, Vermont, which she completed in 2000. Her manuscript for A Step from Heaven, which she produced while earning her degree, was quickly ushered toward publication when her advisor introduced her to his editor. The book was published in 2001. For a time An Na taught middle school, but she has since fully established herself as a professional writer, with her later works including *Wait for Me* (2006) and *The Fold* (2008). She is married and for a time set up a small office in a converted shed in her yard in Kensington, California, in which to write in perfect peace. Most recently, she has been living in Vermont and serving on the faculty of her alma mater, now known as the Vermont College of Fine Arts.

Plot Summary

Sea Bubble—All This Weight—Only God Can

Young Ju overcomes her fear of the deep water as one of her parents holds her while wading in.

Speaking with Young Ju, Halmoni (meaning "Grandmother" ; that is, Young Ju's grandmother) laments that Apa ("Father") needs punishment, as too often he comes home drunk. If Uhmma ("Mother") confronts him, he starts breaking things.

Halmoni teaches Young Ju to pray on behalf of her father. The deceased Harabugi ("Grandfather") is up in heaven, so Young Ju sends her message to God through him.

Mi Gook—Hair—Waiting for Heaven

Young Ju learns from her friend Ju Mi that her family is moving to Mi Gook—America—where Gomo ("Aunt") lives. Young Ju's parents have been talking about Mi Gook at the dinner table. From Uhmma's description of flying, Young Ju gets the impression that "Mi Gook must be in heaven."

Uhmma gets Young Ju's hair curled—an

experience the girl loathes and resents—so that she will fit in among Americans. Young Ju lies and tells her mother she likes her new hair.

Riding in the airplane, Young Ju misses Halmoni. Questioning her mother about heaven, she gets the mistaken impression that Halmoni will be joining them in Mi Gook.

Media Adaptations

- Listening Library produced an audiobook version of *A Step from Heaven* in 2002, read by Jina Oh, with a running time of four hours and fourteen minutes. Originally produced on three audiocassettes, the recording is now available online.

A Step from Heaven—My Future —Not Forever

The family arrives at Gomo's house, and Young Ju looks everywhere for Harabugi. Apa sternly corrects her confusion. Young Ju misses Halmoni even more.

Young Ju attends school and starts to get a better grasp of English. At lunchtime, her teacher gives her goldfish crackers to snack on.

The family moves out of Gomo's house and into their own run-down rental home, in a duplex. When Uhmma objects to the circumstances, Apa slaps her.

Park Joon Ho—Burying Lies— Being Older

In summertime, Gomo is watching over Young Ju, until her parents and Uncle Tim arrive with her new brother, Joon Ho. Apa changes his cherished son's diaper.

At school, Young Ju reports that her brother has died. In response, her teacher gives her stickers and has the class make "warm fuzzies" for her. When the school sends flowers to the family's home, Young Ju, fearing her lie will be discovered, claims they are for getting second in a school spelling bee. She discreetly buries the class's gifts in the yard.

At the fair, Joon Ho loves the balloon his parents bought for him, while Young Ju despises the plastic elephant she won. When Joon Ho accidentally pops his balloon at home, Young Ju gives him the elephant.

Disappearing Bubbles—The Blob —Rainy-Day Surprises

Early in the morning, the sister and brother are gotten out of bed to help wash the car. Apa makes Young Ju work but lets Joon Ho play with bubbles on the ground.

On rare but delightful occasions, Apa sneaks up on his children on weekend mornings to horse around with them, and even with Uhmma.

The children sometimes accompany their mother to her evening restaurant job. In nice weather, they can play in the alley, but when it rains, like this time, they must sit in the car. One time, though, Uhmma brought Young Ju into the kitchen for warm soup and friendly society.

Strong Is a Man—Harry—One Hundred Pennies

Apa orders his children to get ready to go to Gomo's for lunch, but Joon Ho does not want to stop playing with Legos. Apa physically abuses him for his insolence, and furthermore for crying over the abuse.

The siblings find and secretly take care of a baby bird, which they name Harry, but after a week, it dies. They bury it up a hill in a nicer neighborhood.

Young Ju persuades Uhmma to splurge on a dollar lottery ticket. Young Ju dreams of winning, but they get just one of six numbers.

Making Sure—Reaching—My Best Is Always Not Enough

Young Ju accompanies her father to the immigration services office, to renew her green card as she turns thirteen. The father somewhat obtusely insists on receiving confirmation from an employee that they will not have to make another trip.

Young Ju has a recurring dream about reaching for a cloud. A phone call informs the family that Halmoni has died. Apa is disconsolate, but Young Ju tries to comfort him.

Apa is seen sitting late into the night working on the family finances. On a Sunday night, Apa comes home drunk very late, and Uhmma questions him. Apa rages, hits her, and drives away. Now Uhmma—not wearing her wedding ring—is seen working on the finances at night.

The Power of Prayer—Becoming Too American—Punishment

Uhmma, surprisingly, takes the children to

church. Afterward, they go for a sunny winter walk on the beach.

Young Ju's parents will not let her go to her best friend Amanda's birthday party, until they learn that Young Ju borrowed money from her and thus owes her. Afterward, Amanda's parents, the Doyles, drop Young Ju off at a nice home she pretends is her own. At dinner, when Apa says he needs the car and everyone will have to miss church the next day, Young Ju questions him and is slapped for it. He forbids her to see Amanda anymore.

On a Saturday, Gomo and Uncle Tim visit to deliberate over Apa's arrest for drunken driving. The next day, Gomo calls, but Apa makes Uhmma cover for him, and so she insists he come to church. Afterward, tired of all the "punishment," Apa drives away and fails to return home for three days.

Daughter—Revealing Forms—Patches

At the ninth grade's awards ceremony, Young Ju earns the prize for highest grade point average. The Doyles drive her to the library near her home, passing through a police checkpoint on the way. Later, Uhmma declares she is very proud. Apa fails to take note of the certificate.

On a Sunday morning, Young Ju realizes from her mother's uncharacteristic behavior that something is wrong. In the trash, she and Joon Ho find an empty liquor bottle and ten beer cans. Going inside to Uhmma, Young Ju sees the bruises on her back. She confronts her mother about making choices.

Joon Ho has been skipping school. Young Ju, who has received the school's calls, threatens to tell their parents.

Disclosure—Seeds of Life—A Family of Dreamers

Young Ju has been discreetly, but increasingly often, hanging out with Amanda. She returns home one day and is confronted by Apa, who saw her getting out of the Doyles's car. She lies, and he starts beating her. When Uhmma intervenes, Apa turns brutally toward her. The terrifying commotion eventually motivates Young Ju to call 911 and plead for help.

After being treated at the hospital, Uhmma and Young Ju go to pick Apa up from the police station —but he leaves in the car of another woman instead. Uhmma starts working three jobs, and Young Ju and Joon Ho take on more chores and start working at Uncle Tim's icecream shop. One night, Uhmma comes home during her work break to say that Apa is going back to Korea—but they will stay in America.

Uhmma and her children settle into their new home, purchased with recently earned money and help from Gomo and Tim in the form of a loan. Young Ju is soon going to college. She finds old family photographs, including one of her on the beach—it was her father who held her, waded into the water, and taught her not to be afraid.

Epilogue: Hands

Young Ju describes Uhmma's work-weathered hands, and how she used to read the lines on her children's palms. Uhmma and Young Ju walk along the beach and speak of the mother's scars.

Characters

Apa

See Park Byung Ho

John Chuchurelli

John is a classmate of Young Ju's in elementary school.

Cook

The Chinese cook at Johnny's Steak House makes a special impression on Young Ju when her mother brings her into the kitchen.

Amanda Doyle

The girl who gives Young Ju a Lifesaver candy upon learning the (invented) news of her brother's death becomes Young Ju's best friend throughout their high school years.

Mr. and Mrs. Doyle

Amanda's parents are very encouraging of Young Ju and want to befriend her parents as well, but Young Ju is too ashamed of her family's dysfunction and relative poverty to ever let the well-off Doyles see where she actually lives.

Gomo

Gomo is Apa's sister. Her residence in the United States gives Apa and Uhmma a connection for their own immigrating, and Gomo helps support them by providing a temporary place to live. Unfortunately, either she is not involved enough in her brother's life to realize that he is abusive, or she accepts such abuse as part of a patriarchal culture. When Gomo opens her own laundry business, Uhmma works there, which eventually enables Uhmma and her children to buy their own home.

Grill Woman

The Japanese woman who works the grill at the steak house seems to be a close friend of Uhmma's, even though they can speak only to each other in a simplified combination of Korean, Japanese, and English.

Halmoni

Young Ju's grandmother stays behind in Korea when her son's family moves to the United States. Young Ju misses her very much, but they do not see Halmoni again before she dies, about ten years later.

Harabugi

Harabugi is Apa's father—Young Ju's paternal

grandfather. He is already deceased when the novel begins.

Ju Mi

Ju Mi, who is Young Ju's older friend back in Korea, is the one to break the news to her about the Park family's move to America.

Mr. and Mrs. Kim

The minister at Grace Church and his wife are very kind to Uhmma, but Apa resents the special attention they give him when he finally shows up alongside her.

Kimberly

The white waitress at the steak house brings Uhmma and her daughter special drinks—Shirley Temples, which are nonalcoholic cocktails.

Mr. Owner

The man who owns the duplex in which the Parks live is known to Young Ju simply as Mr. Owner.

Park Byung Ho

Called Apa by his daughter, Byung Ho's name is revealed only when his sister, Gomo, scolds him after his arrest for drunken driving. A fisherman back in Korea, Apa proves disappointed with the move to America, where he must work not only as a gardener but also cleaning lawyers' offices. He resents having to share living space with his sister and her husband, so he insists that he and Uhmma rent their own apartment—even though this makes their financial situation worse and delays their ability to buy their own home. Pigheaded and self-righteous, he drinks, smokes, and physically abuses anyone in the family who disagrees with him, wife, daughter, and son alike. The reader cannot be surprised when it turns out that he has been spending his time away with another woman, and when he decides to return to Korea, it is clear that his family will be better off without him.

Park Joon Ho

Young Ju's little brother is in some ways spoiled by Apa, who clearly perceives a son as a far more important person than a daughter. Yet Apa's high expectations for his young son's level of manliness backfire: when Apa tries to correct Joon Ho's juvenile insolence and emotionality with violence, Joon Ho simply starts hating him. By his teenage years, Joon Ho seems to be going off the rails. He skips school routinely, and the changes Young Ju sees in his face suggest that he is experimenting, perhaps dangerously, with alcohol or drugs. Apa's departure is undoubtedly good for him; getting a steady job at Kinko's, Joon Ho helps his mother and sister pay for their new home.

Park Suna

Called Uhmma by her children, Suna's name is revealed when she converses with her coworkers at the roadside restaurant. Originally from a well-to-do family, she has had to avoid mentioning her relatives to avoid annoying her husband. Uhmma is devoted to her children and to her husband—arguably too much to Apa, because even when he starts abusing his daughter as well as herself, she is unable to make a difficult decision (namely, leaving Apa) to preserve their wellbeing. In fact, when Young Ju finally calls 911 to report the episode of abuse that might well have proved lethal, Uhmma actually scolds Young Ju for breaking up the family. After reflection, however, Uhmma is able to thank Young Ju for doing the right thing.

Park Young Ju

Young Ju (Park is her family name; in Korean, it appears before her given name) is the novel's protagonist and narrator. The reader gets profound insight into Young Ju's mind because her thought processes are tracked from a very early age—four or younger—all the way through her adolescence and into her young adulthood. The move to America distresses her primarily because they must leave behind the beloved Halmoni, who has been a refuge of care and safety for Young Ju whenever her father's drunkenness made the nuclear family unstable. Subsequently, she must navigate life as a young immigrant in America practically on her own, eventually becoming the translator for her parents as they deal with official matters. She is highly perceptive, but Apa's domineering ways make it difficult for her to achieve a level of assertiveness in her own life. She must overcome a great deal of hesitation before calling the police on Apa, even as he takes his violent impulses to an extreme. The results of that call are at first mixed, but the passage of time makes clear that the event was a pivotal one in Young Ju's life: having decisively rebelled against her tyrannical father, she took her family's collective life, and her own, into her own hands.

Sahmchun

See Uncle Tim

Mrs. Sheldon

Young Ju's second-grade teacher must respond on the fly to the (inaccurate) news of Young Ju's brother's death. She is very sympathetic.

Mr. Shin

The youth minister at Uhmma's church is Mr. Shin.

Mrs. Song

Mrs. Song is a fellow congregation member with whom Uhmma gets rides to church when necessary—though she insists that she and her children walk the several miles to Mrs. Song's house rather than be picked up by her.

Spencer

Spencer is the friend with whom Joon Ho is playing Legos on the day Apa ends up punishing his son abusively.

Uncle Tim

Gomo's American husband rarely steps out of the background of the novel. He owns a tiny icecream shop at the beach, where he employs Young Ju and Joon Ho when Apa's departure puts the family in financial straits. The fact that he discourages Gomo from speaking Korean at home, since he does not understand it, does not reflect well on him; a more open-minded and compassionate husband would make an effort to learn his wife's native language.

Uhmma

See Park Suna

Themes

Immigrant Life

An Na's novel provides great insight into the sorts of issues affecting not only Korean immigrants in America but also immigrants from everywhere. A move to a new country is often intended as a new start in life, and America is famous worldwide for being the land of opportunity—and yet this does not necessarily mean that the opportunities offered are ideal for everyone. As the novel opens, the Park family is leading a humble existence in South Korea, living off of Apa's work as a fisherman, and so America would seem to give them a chance to improve their lives. However, to begin with, they must leave the beloved Halmoni behind, taking away a pillar of emotional support for Young Ju, not to mention a source of reliable and trustworthy child care. Once in America, starting out in poverty, they must live with a relative, Gomo, and give up some of their privacy. Moving into their own apartment is not much of an improvement, since they gain privacy but lose a great deal of money to monthly rent. Moreover, the apartment itself is in very poor condition. When Apa must get a job as a custodian, he grows even more resentful of the move to America. He liked his job as a fisherman, humble though it was; it seems that Uhmma was the one who considered life as a fisherman's wife too humble, as she once specifically expresses her hope that Young Ju will end up with a better life than hers. In the meantime, Young Ju must deal with her own immigrant's problems, such as not knowing the language, having to cope with her parents' not knowing the language, and not feeling as if she can fit in with wealthier, white classmates.

The drawbacks of immigrating to America for a family like the Parks seem to so outweigh the benefits that one might think they made the wrong decision. And yet the payoff turns out to be there: Young Ju not only gets a decent education but excels academically, and a wellpaying, and hopefully satisfying, professional career is likely on the horizon. The parents themselves may not personally benefit from the move, but they made sacrifices specifically for their children. A question that remains is whether it was worth ultimately sacrificing the unity of the family for the sake of the children's future.

Sex Roles

One of the issues that confronts the Parks is that of the gendered roles that boys and girls are expected to play. With the women's rights movement of the early twentieth century and the several waves of feminism since then, marked by legislation ranging from the Nineteenth Amendment (for women's right to vote) to Title IX (for equal opportunities in men's and women's collegiate athletics), the United States is among the nations at the forefront of achieving true gender equality in society. It may lag behind more progressive nations like those in Scandinavia, but in comparison to traditional Korean society—at least as depicted in An Na's novel—the difference is stark. That is, Apa is suggested to have a traditionally Korean outlook with regard to masculinity and femininity: men are the stronger ones and thus get more privileges, while women are supposed to be subordinate to their fathers and husbands. Apa insists that his wife and daughter obey him, and if they even question his orders, he abuses them. Apa blames Young Ju's American friend Amanda for instilling in her too great a sense of independence, leading him to forbid her to see Amanda at all. Around the world, many traditional cultures have retained patriarchal social orders that depend upon the submission and subordination of women. This is not to say that all men within such cultures take advantage of that order to become tyrannical husbands and fathers, but An Na's novel makes clear that tyranny is a distinct possibility within such a culture, allowing monsters like Apa to flourish.

Topics for Further Study

- Using narration revolving around a child's perspective, An Na includes little description of environment or scenery in *A Step from Heaven*, and thus nature plays a very minor role —in fact, primarily a metaphorical role. Reread the novel seeking out references, however brief, to aspects of nature, and write a paper analyzing the role that such references play and what they say about the significance of nature in Young Ju's life.

- Familiar yourself with Lawrence Kohlberg's stage theory of moral development. (As a starting point, the online *Encyclopædia Britannica* has a concise summary of the topic.)

Write a paper in which you discuss Young Ju's moral development over the course of *A Step from Heaven*, identifying stages she passes through wherever possible. In closing, discuss whether you think Kohlberg's theory suffices to fully account for Young Ju's personal, individual sense of morality.

- Read the young-adult novel *Since You Asked* (2015), by Maurene Goo, which follows Americanized fifteen-year-old Holly Kim as she copes with her traditional parents' expectations—in part by writing about them in a school newspaper column. Imagine that the teenage Young Ju, prior to her father's departure from the family, reads a few of Holly's columns, and produce two documents: one being a letter that Young Ju writes to Holly expressing her difficulties at home, and the other being a column that Holly writes to give advice and encouragement to Young Ju and others in similar situations.

- Using online resources including text and video, teach yourself to both speak and write a number of words in Korean. If you know anyone in your school or community who speaks Korean, you might politely ask him or her for a small amount of assistance with pronunciation and handwriting. (Alternatively, if you already speak Korean, prepare a brief lesson on words and phrases that would be of interest to your classmates. Include ways in which the language differs from English.) Then create a presentation, using a tool such as PowerPoint or Prezi, in order to give your classmates a basic lesson in Korean.

Dysfunctional Families

The situation of the Park family is a heartrending one. Making the move to America seems like a solution to less-than-ideal circumstances, but Apa has violent, drunken tendencies even before the move, and it can be little surprise that this continues in America. In fact, the constraints of immigrant life—the work he does not like, the unpleasant apartment, the place of women in American society, and surely also the lack of a communal support structure—bring out the worst in him. Although Halmoni laments, before the move, that she can no longer control Apa, she likely at least subdued his worst impulses simply through her presence. In her absence, there is no meaningful authority figure in his life whatsoever.

The Park family descends into dysfunction. They lack money, but Apa insists that they rent their own apartment instead of sharing; to pay the rent, they need to save money more than ever, but Apa wastes even more money on alcohol to cope with all the stress. Even when he starts beating Uhmma, she has so few people to turn to—she has no blood relatives in America—that the only option she can perceive is to suffer silently. It is the Americanized Young Ju who finally helps her out of this quagmire. The reader can see, then, that while immigration might have brought the Park family to this unfortunate crisis of dysfunction, going through the crisis is what allows them to emerge on the other side, giving Apa the freedom he apparently needed all along and the rest of the family the freedom from Apa that they needed in turn.

Parent-Child Relationships

The Park family has so much difficulty and negativity to work through that the novel itself becomes very weighty—so weighty that the reader yearns for some positivity to balance the tone. And, indeed, there is a bright spot, in the relationship between mother and daughter that develops after Apa returns to Korea. Uhmma was suffering and could not see a way out, perhaps because she had been subordinated by her traditional culture for so long. Young Ju comes to perceive her mother's suffering, through the bruises on her body and especially the cries that fill the air when Apa brutally attacks her. Young Ju's love for her mother is what inspires her to finally take the necessary step outside of the tyrannical authority of the father and summon a higher authority—the American police—to put an end to his abuse. In the book's epilogue, Young Ju laments that she had not been able to prevent her mother's hands from becoming scarred by all the cleaning and cooking and laundering she has had to do all her life, but Uhmma's response is an affirmative one: she has lived her life with all her strength, for her daughter's sake. She is not ashamed of her scarred hands but proud of what she has enabled her daughter to accomplish in her own life.

Style

Child Narrator

An Na proves masterly at writing from the perspective of a child, and not merely at a particular age but at the full range of ages from the toddler years up through young adulthood. The narration of the opening chapter is striking in its descriptive minimalism, elementary sentence structure, and impressionistic images. In fact, the chapter consists entirely of dialogue, reflecting, to begin with, how such a young child lacks the self-awareness needed to provide a running account of what is going in one's existence. The child simply *is*, and in the absence of an internal monologue, all that can be recorded of the child's experiences are the comments spoken aloud. Appropriately, the comments spoken by the child lack the full grammatical complement that would make them clear to a reader or listener. Thus, she says only "Cold water," instead of "This water is cold," and "Tickles," instead of "That tickles." The chapter does conclude with italicized words that suggest that this sort of formative experience is precisely what leads the child to have enough self-consciousness to express thoughts internally—in this case, her whimsically imagined identity as a bubble.

The child's perspective is significant in

multiple succeeding episodes, with An Na heightening the visceral feel of the drama by using the present tense throughout. Reflecting her limited grasp of the idea of saltwater, as well as a natural grasp of metaphor, Young Ju mentions that when her father breaks things, her "eyes bleed water from the sea." Although modern adults "know better" than to believe in magic, Young Ju can recognize that *Mi Gook* "is a magic word" for her parents because of the way it instantly gives rise to positive possibilities in their minds. Another fascinating episode revolves around Young Ju's report to her class that her brother is dead. Children do not necessarily understand that if they declare something that does not match reality, this means that they are "lying." Young Ju is, of course, really only imagining for the day that her brother is dead, because she thinks her life would be better that way; her conscience never kicks into gear even as she is being showered with gifts of condolence from her classmates. It is only when she recognizes that her parents would be angry if they knew what she said, and that she would be punished, that she fully realizes that she has done something wrong. This accurately reflects the way children begin to ethically develop.

Bilingual Literature

More and more through the end of the twentieth century and beginning of the twenty-first, American writers with international backgrounds have leaned toward producing English-language novels peppered with words in a different language. Given the proximity of Latin America, this most often occurs with Spanish, such as in works by the likes of Julia Alvarez and Junot Díaz. Where earlier generations were more likely to provide only foreign terms in conjunction with some means of translation—either within the narrative or in a glossary—present-day writers often take the apparently riskier tactic of providing no translation, sometimes not even contextually. Thus, a reader of a Díaz novel who speaks no Spanish will not fully understand every sentence without looking up the vocabulary.

Much rarer is a bilingual novel featuring English and Korean. The Korean hangul script is of course entirely separate from the Roman alphabet used in English, and so the Korean words in *A Step from Heaven* are actually *transliterated*, meaning that the spelling in the Roman alphabet reproduces the sound of the original. As such, the spellings of An Na's Korean terms do not necessarily match what an online translator would provide. Nonetheless, one can determine that the names used for Young Ju's relatives are indeed the words that describe the relation. *Apa* is not a name but the word for "father" or "papa." In turn, *uhmma* means "mother" or "mama," *halmoni* means "grandmother," *sahmchun* means "uncle," and so forth. An Na does use a few terms where the meaning is less clear. For example, *ahjimma* seems to be a term for an adult woman, while *uhn-nee* seem to mean an older sibling, but neither term's meaning is perfectly obvious.

Special insight into language differences is provided when An Na presents dialogue as five or six-year-old Young Ju hears people speak English at school while she knows only Korean herself. By the spellings provided, Young Ju seems to literally not hear *l* sounds, some *h* sounds in combination, and *r* and *t* sounds at the ends of words—sounds presumably not naturally present in Korean. Thus, *All right class, come over here* sounds to her like "Ah ri cas, ca mo ve he" ; *Welcome* becomes "Wah ko um" ; *This is Young* becomes "Tees es Yung" ; and *Goldfish* becomes "Go-do-feesh." English speakers who have tried to learn a second language have likely experienced this same phenomenon in reverse; certain sounds in a foreign language lack any full correlation to English sounds, making it impossible to accurately spell out foreign words merely from hearing them spoken. By presenting Young Ju's natural interpretation of English syllables, An Na allows the reader greater empathy with regard to immigrants' challenges in adapting to immersion and education in a foreign language.

Koreans in America

Korean Americans, including both those who immigrated from Korea and those born in the United States to Korean parents, have a shared experience distinct from those of other Asian Americans. Although they have often come at different times and for different reasons than other Asian immigrants, sociologist Moon H. Jo observes that Americans generally "are not adept in differentiating Koreans from Chinese, Japanese, or other Asian groups," which has contributed to a lack of popular knowledge of Korean Americans' circumstances.

There have been three major waves of Korean immigration to the United States. The first wave began in the wake of legislation passed in 1882, when xenophobic fears on the part of white Americans, which eventually gave birth to the racist term *yellow peril*, prompted the Chinese Exclusion Act. Chinese laborers became scarce on Hawaiian plantations, and by early 1902 Koreans were immigrating in their stead. (Hawaii was not yet a state, but it had become a US Territory in 1898.) Conditions on plantations and in the other jobs available to unskilled workers in Hawaii were not ideal, but Korea had been experiencing famine, a cholera epidemic, increased taxation, and government corruption. Korean immigration increased further when the Japanese were gradually excluded in the first decade of the twentieth century, but all immigration from the East was throttled by the Immigration Act of 1924, which allowed only one hundred people from any given Asian country to enter America each year. The second wave of Korean immigration came with the outbreak of the Korean War in 1951, which led to America's admittance of numerous orphaned children, students, and wives of servicemen. The third wave came after President Lyndon Johnson's Immigration Act of 1965 effectively abolished the quotas. If Young Ju's life is seen as historically aligning with An Na's own, the protagonist's family would have entered the United States as part of this wave, in the mid-1970s.

The 1965 act led to a boom in the Korean American population. Numbering 70,000 in 1970, the population quintupled in just a decade, reaching over 357,000 in 1980. The population more than doubled again over the following decade, to over 787,000 in 1990. As Jo notes, somewhat ironically, one disadvantage for Koreans in America, in comparison to those from India, the Philippines, and Hong Kong, has been the fact that they had no exposure to colonization and thus, in general, little familiarity with the English language. (Generally, colonial influences on colonized countries were, and remain, damaging.) With smaller immigrant communities than Japanese and Chinese Americans, Koreans have had less of a support network. Describing the most pressing issues faced by

Koreans in America, Jo effectively lists the major themes in An Na's novel: "Among the most frequently mentioned difficulties of adaptation … are the language barrier, finding a means of earning a living, family stresses, social isolation, cultural conflict, and the consequences of their children's education." Koreans met with news-making conflict especially in the closing decades of the twentieth century, when Korean grocery store owners in New York, Los Angeles, and other urban centers variously clashed, broadly speaking, with black customers, Latino employees, and white suppliers.

In *Koreans in North America*, Pyong Gap Min points out that one important means of Korean Americans' supporting each other has been religion, with three-quarters of immigrants being affiliated with either Protestant or Catholic churches with primarily Korean congregations. And yet Jo observes that the insulated nature of these congregations has contributed to relatively slow processes of adaptation, especially for older generations, who tend to exhibit "strong ethnocentrism" :

> Socially,… most Korean immigrants have not been able to free themselves from the protective circle of their Korean friends and relatives. Their tendency to limit their association to Koreans whom they have met at church, at work, and at social gatherings further delays their assimilation process.

On a more promising note, Jo relates that Korean Americans raised in the United States tend to have a better experience than new immigrants in learning the language, understanding social customs, and meeting with integrative success in their professional and personal lives.

Critical Overview

A Step from Heaven attracted widespread critical and popular attention both before and after it was nominated for the National Book Award and won the Printz Award. Upon the book's release, *Publishers Weekly* described it in a starred review as a "mesmerizing" novel narrated in "fluid, lyrical language" by a "graceful and resonant voice." The reviewer considers the plot "consistently absorbing," as "the narrative unfolds through jewel-like moments carefully strung together." The book is seen to ultimately portray for its protagonist a "future full of hope. Equally bright are the prospects of this author.'

Attracting the attention of the *New York Times Book Review*, the novel inspired Susan Chira to call it an "engaging tale … endowed with a haunting grace by the exquisite voice of a new young writer." Though culturally specific in many ways, the book is seen to have "universal resonance." Chira is especially impressed with the qualities of protagonist Young Ju: "A wonderful character she is: feisty, observant, empathetic, and resourceful. … Her struggle to endure, and finally to rebel, makes a book full of heartbreaking scenes become, in the end, a story of triumph."

Horn Book also offered a starred review of the novel, noting that the concise chapters "have the intimacy of snapshots," while the protagonist's voice "is convincingly articulated." The reviewer concludes that "each of these vignettes by first-time author An Na displays an astonishing and memorable force." Similarly, Hazel Rochman, in *Booklist*, observes that each vignette is "a story in itself," and they all "blend together into a beautiful coming-of-age drama" that will prove both absorbing and thoughtprovoking for teenage readers. In *Kliatt*, Ann Hart admires how An Na never bogs down the apt focus on the present moment with longwinded backstories or extensive description of scenery and so forth. In Hart's words, the book features "no burdensome narrative, which makes it appealing for younger readers with short attention spans. The manner and sensitivity of the storytelling itself will appeal to all readers." Hart concludes that *A Step from Heaven* is "a welcome addition to Asian American literature," and speaking on behalf of critics and readers young and old alike, she declares, "We will eagerly await more from this author."

Compare & Contrast

- **ca. 2000:** As of 2000, there are approximately 1.23 million Americans of at least partial Korean descent. Of those, 1.1 million are of only Korean heritage.

  Today: As of 2010, there are some 1.7 million Korean Americans, with just over 1.4 million claiming full

Korean heritage.

- **ca. 2000:** If a teenager's parents forbid her to spend time with a friend, it can be hard to arrange meetings outside of school hours, since phone conversations at home are liable to be overheard.

  Today: With a majority of teenagers using their own cell phones, meetings can be easily arranged either by bringing one's phone outside the house for conversations or simply by texting.

- **ca. 2000:** With the South Korean economy hit especially hard by Asia's 1997 financial crisis, the nation is forced to take loans from the International Monetary Fund, leading president Kim Dae-jung to announce a national effort to increase income by exporting its culture, in what is dubbed *hallyu*, meaning "Korean wave."

  Today: Globally, Korean culture has become, in a word, cool, especially in the form of Korean pop music, or "K-pop." In the 2010s, rapper Psy makes international waves with the hit song "Gangnam Style" (2012), and songs by girl group 2NE1 are featured in Samsung and Microsoft advertisements.

What Do I Read Next?

- An Na's second young-adult novel, *Wait for Me* (2006), follows Korean American teenager Mina, who faces pressure from her parents to succeed academically but has secretly been stashing away money in order to move into her own apartment after high school instead of attending Harvard. As a further complication, she falls in love with Ysrael, a Mexican immigrant.

- Another acclaimed Korean American writer is Chang-Rae Lee. Having earned admiring reviews with his first novel *Native Speaker*

(1995), about a Korean American in New York City going through a crisis in both his marriage and his espionage work, Lee took on a more historically ambitious project with *The Surrendered* (2010), about the impact the Korean War had on the lives of ordinary Koreans.

- An Na has specifically cited Sandra Cisneros's *The House on Mango Street* (1984) as an important influence on her own debut. Cisneros's novel treats the adolescence of Esperanza, a Latina girl living in Chicago, through a series of vignettes that are almost short stories in and of themselves.

- One of the teachers at Vermont College whom An Na has especially praised as a mentor is Jacqueline Woodson, herself an accomplished writer for young-adult audiences. One of Woodson's most acclaimed titles is *Brown Girl Dreaming* (2013), winner of the National Book Award for youth literature and several additional awards. *Brown Girl Dreaming* is a novel in verse that begins with protagonist Jacqueline's childhood in South Carolina.

- Praised by An Na as one of her

favorite authors when she was younger, Beverly Cleary has written dozens of well-known titles, especially featuring the character of Ramona Quimby. *Ramona and Her Father* (1977) finds Ramona developing a new relationship with her father when he loses his job and copes in part by smoking cigarettes, a habit Ramona detests.

- An Na is one of the contributors to the multicultural anthology *No Such Thing as the Real World: Stories about Growing Up and Getting a Life* (2009), which also features stories by Woodson, M. T. Anderson, K. L. Going, Beth Kephart, and Chris Lynch.

- A fantasy action novel that draws on Korean folklore for its mythological setting is *Prophecy* (2013), by Ellen Oh. This book, the first in a series, follows warrior girl Kira as she tries to protect a prince from a demon invasion.

- Bong-youn Choy's long work *Koreans in America* (1979) features extensive discussion of the historical relationship that Korea and Koreans had with the United States and Americans. The first chapter provides an introduction to Korean history and culture.

Sources

Chira, Susan, Review of *A Step from Heaven*, in *New York Times Book Review*, May 20, 2001, p. S22.

Hart, Ann, Review of *A Step from Heaven*, in *Kliatt*, Vol. 37, No. 2, March 2003, p. 25.

Hoeffel, Elizabeth M., Sonya Rastogi, Myoung Ouk Kim, and Hasan Shahid, "The Asian Population: 2010," US Census Bureau, March 2012, https://www.census.gov/prod/cen2010/briefs/c2010t 11.pdf (accessed May 23, 2017).

"Interview with Young Adult Author An Na," Cynthia Leitich Smith website, December 2001, http://cynthialeitichsmith.com/lit-resources/read/authors/interviews/anna/ (accessed May 21, 2017).

J. M. B., Review of *A Step from Heaven*, in *Horn Book*, Vol. 77, No. 4, July 2001, p. 458.

Jo, Moon H., *Korean Immigrants and the Challenge of Adjustment*, pp. xi–xix, 1–18.

Min, Pyong Gap, ed., Introduction to *Koreans in North America; Their Twenty-First Century Experiences*, Lexington Books, 2013, pp. 1–8.

Parker, Derek, "The Korean Invasion," *American Interest*, February 9, 2015, https://www.the-american-interest.com/2015/02/09/the-korean-invasion/ (accessed May 23, 2017).

Review of *A Step from Heaven*, in *Publishers Weekly*, Vol. 248, No. 14, April 2, 2001, p. 65.

Rochman, Hazel, Review of *A Step from Heaven*, in *Booklist*, Vol. 98, No. 6, November 15, 2001, p. 567.

Further Reading

Choi, Yearn Hong, and Haeng Ja Kim, *Surfacing Sadness: A Centennial of Korean-American Literature, 1903–2003*, Homa & Sekey Books, 2003.

> This anthology presents poetry, short stories, and essays written by a variety of Korean American authors, including works originally written in English as well as works translated from Korean.

Forward, Susan, and Craig Buck, *Toxic Parents: Overcoming Their Hurtful Legacy and Reclaiming Your Life*, Random House, 2009.

> This text primarily written by Dr. Forward—also author of *Men Who Hate Women and the Women Who Love Them*—is intended as a guide for those who have dealt with parental abuse and are seeking to overcome its lasting psychological impact.

Hong, Eugy, *The Birth of Korean Cool: How One Nation Is Conquering the World through Pop Culture*, Picador, 2014.

> Although the focus of this text is Korean pop culture, Hong delves into the economic, political, and

historical factors that have combined to set Korea up for its present-day relationship with global society.

Kingston, Maxine Hong, *The Woman Warrior: Memoirs of a Girlhood among Ghosts*, Alfred A. Knopf, 1976.

Among the books that An Na has cited as influences is Kingston's groundbreaking work of literature, which uses poetic language and imaginings to describe the author's experiences growing up in a Chinese family in California.

Suggested Search Terms

An Na AND A Step from Heaven

An Na AND young-adult literature

Korean American literature

Korean American history

Koreans AND Christianity

Korean language AND hangul

immigrant challenges AND English language

alcohol AND parental abuse

Korea AND patriarchy

Korea AND hallyu